WHEN HURT

HITS

EBONY BROWN

DEDICATION

First and foremost, I'm giving God the honor because He has been so good to me and never left my side through my good and bad days, always making a way even when I wanted to give up.

"The Lord himself goes before you and will be with you; he will never leave you nor forsake you. Do not be afraid; Do not be discourage."

— *Deuteronomy 3 1:8.*

To my parents, what would I have done without your love and strong support throughout the years? From days I thought I was worthless to days when I thought no one could have told me anything, no matter what it was, you both were still there.

And to my wonderful, most amazing kids, y'all are my reasons why I do what I do. Y'all give me life, courage, patience, understanding, motivation, and true love. Y'all make me feel like a true superwoman. Mama got y'all I promise. MY LUCKY 4

WHEN HURT HITS

I t all started as being high school sweethearts as we met inside Spanish class at Garrett Academy of Technology. I was in eleventh grade, and JR was in tenth grade. Sitting inside a class, I noticed this handsome, baby-faced young man eyeing me, but I never thought anything of it. As a couple of Spanish classes went by, JR wanted our classmate to get my number for him. I was the shy type of girl, so all I did was laugh it off. Class ended, and a homegirl of mine gave JR my number without me even knowing, although she told me after the fact. What I did was laugh, not really caring because he was cute, and I wanted to see what he was all about. We had A/B days, so JR and I didn't see each other as much unless I would see him walking through the hallways. Some days passed by, and I received a text saying, "wuz up, sweetheart," I did not think it would have been JR, and also thought, well, this can't be my boyfriend because this isn't his number, and he doesn't approach me as a sweetheart. So I replied, "Who is this." Along the line, the person then replied, "JR from Spanish class." Me trying to act cool but nervous, I replied, "oh wuz up," with a BIG smile.

JR and I chatted through text for a little that day. As days continued to pass by, I and JR started chopping it up with each other every day, trying to get to know each other. I was in a Lil six-month relationship at the time. However, it was something about JR I started to fall for, so honestly, my relationship with this other dude eventually faded away. Everything started so lovely between me and JR; we started hanging out together almost every day after school.

When his parents brought JR his first car, he would pick me up for school in the mornings and drop me off home after. On the days I didn't have to work, we would walk in the park, grab something to eat, or even sit in his car parked somewhere and talk for hours.

JR had me thinking, damn, am I the only one who was JUST a thought. It was like I and JR clicked so perfectly together, more like being in love at first sight. JR was one of the most handsome, popular boys around the school, so he was the flirtatious, hoe type. JR really couldn't fool me, but being so young and dumb and knowing deep down inside I wasn't the only one, I would just ignore the fact of what I was assuming because I had no evidence just yet. JR started to spoil me; he would buy me all types of jewelry, give me lunch money, and keep me with a new pair of shoe nahhh. I'm guessing that was his little cover-up for me not to think he was all mixed up with all types of females. JR was a street nigga, so yes, he did sell drugs.

Burger King was my first job in high school, where I worked from eleventh grade up to the end of summer after graduating. Being with a street nigga came with so much stress, overthinking, sacrificing, and even worries, but I didn't care. I was really feeling dude. JR would take Lil losses here and there (drug losses), and I would literally give this boy my entire check for him to get back straight. I looked at it like this shoot; he looks out for me, so why wouldn't I return the favor? And he also knew I would have been there for him through whatever. The first time I and JR had sex was at my mother's house, where I snuck him in one night, not knowing we would sleep the night away. My mother found us laid up beside my bed on the floor the next day. I then heard a voice whispering, "Ebony" Whewwww, I woke up scared; thank God it wasn't my father. My mother asked JR "what are you doing in my house? Ebony, did y'all have sex?" I said, "no, mama."

I felt so dumb telling my mother no because I knew she knew I was lying deep down inside. My mother didn't act like our friend to my siblings and me, but she was the laid-back, forgiving type that would be there for us no matter what. She helped me sneak JR back out of the house from my father and took JR home. The whole ride to JR's house was complete silence; that was my mother's first time meeting JR. Me and JR's first Thanksgiving together was when I finally met JR's family. The vibe was so laid back and full of laughter; everyone made me feel so comfortable. I felt like I actually fitted in, but you know, there's always that one person who clowns around out of every family.

One of his cousins made a joke about me saying," JR, she is beautiful, but she looks crazy as hell," INFRONT OF EVERYONE. He caught me off guard; it was funny and embarrassing at the same time. As time went by, things started to change slightly as I fell deeper and deeper in love with JR. We would get into little arguments here and there about my suspicions about him messing around. JR was the type that hated me talking back to him in arguments like I was his child or something. Arguments eventually turned into fights. After school on school grounds, our first fight took place when I finally confronted him about a female he was talking to. I had proof, I saw it on his phone, but he tried to lie about it as we were arguing. JR suddenly started choking me and then backhanded me as he called me a "dumb ass bitch." We fought; although JR was this skinny-built type of nigga, he was strong. I cried so bad that day, never thinking a day like this would have come from being in a relationship, especially me being so young and eyes puffy and bloodshot red. I was getting worried because I couldn't go home just yet; I couldn't let my parents see me in this predicament, so I hid at JR's sister's house until night fell when I knew my mother was in bed. My mother really had no worries about my whereabouts because she knew JR would be the only person I would have been with every day after school. As I got home that night, washed up, and got ready for bed for school the next morning, I received a text from JR. "man sweetheart, I'm sorry I flipped out, you had me shittin, them bitches don't mean nothing to me, I promise I won't ever put my hands on you again." Excuses upon excuses, but yes, I dumbly accepted his apology, and we made up that next day, and things went back to normal. As you can see, apologies always come in gift form like gifting flowers, jewelry, or even a vacation out of town ending with sex. I had two homegirls I really fucked with at school that also had boyfriends that attended Garret; while we three hung out together, our boyfriends also hung out together. My homegirls and I would always get together and have conversations about our relationship problems and what we would be going through, and we tried to give our best advice to each other. I would be too embarrassed about my stories, but I felt comfortable sharing them with them because we never judged each other's decisions or pain. We were so close and more like sisters; we all had so much in common. Both of my homegirls ended up pregnant in high school, I wouldn't say I wanted to follow them, but I wanted a baby from JR deep down inside. Me being in twelfth grade at the time, I thought I was grown enough to handle my own decisions, so I ended up getting off of birth control. JR and I tried to get pregnant, but it wasn't happening for us. I started to get discouraged and gave up having thoughts to myself, could this be a sign, or maybe it's not my time, or if I could even produce kids. The time has come. Graduation day!!! I was so excited for this day to come, and I wouldn't say I liked high school; I wanted to be on my own and do what I wanted to do, not knowing how hard life could be as a young adult. As a graduation gift, my parents brought me my first car, a 2003 grey ford Taurus, and I was so appreciative of it. Straight out of high school that summer of 2009, I applied for my first apartment in Hanahan, South Carolina, where I attended Trident Technical College, minutes away from where I stayed. I've always had dreams and visions of being a nurse, and I was focused. One month later, I found out I was pregnant with my first child. I was in disbelief to the extent that I took five pregnancy tests; it was unbelievable that I really was pregnant. I was happy. Eight weeks into my pregnancy, I started to get entirely sick to the point that I couldn't do anything or function the right way, so I had to withdraw from school. I then felt like my dreams had just gone down the drain. I also lost my apartment due to not being able to work any longer to afford my bills. I then had no choice but to let my parents know about my situation and move back home. I was so blessed to have such understanding and helpful parents that had no problem taking me back in. Five months into my pregnancy, this nigga really tried to fight me. JR took too long with some food. I had to ask him to bring me, so I called him and got no answer. I started to blow JR's phone up, calling back to back constantly; at this point, I was getting frustrated. He finally answered, fussing back and forth; after being told for hours he was coming, JR finally pulled up to my mother's house. He called me outside; I got in the car, and as he started to back up out the yard, he made a complete stop. JR then says, "Now, I ain't taking you anywhere again because you have been blocking my serves from calling me messing up my money." Me having this blank stare on my face like JR, you came all the way over here hours later just to do this. And you were driving MY car, my shit. JR had sold his car, so I was nice enough to let him use mine whenever he wanted it. At this point, I wanted to cry. I was shittin, and I was hungry. I said, "I'm not going a damn where." So my stubborn behind stayed right inside the car. He then got out of the car, came around to my side, opened the door, and pulled on me, trying to get me out. As I was pulling back from him, trying to get him off of me, I didn't want to take it to another level because, unfortunately, he didn't care about me being pregnant. I knew he would have taken it too far. He forcefully jerked me out of the car as I fell on the wet, muddy ground and left me there. I didn't hear from JR until the next day; he called me like nothing had just happened last night. Knowing I was settling for less than what I deserved and realizing having a child from a man doesn't hold any type of weight, I still managed to give JR a chance. After sitting home for nine months, plus after giving birth to my son, I realized it was time for me to get myself back together and get back on track with my life. Also, having a big responsibility for my head and still thinking that I still needed to be there for JR, I had to get myself together. What if he needed me financially? What if he fell short on something? I then attended school to become a Certified Nurse.

Worked as an after-school councilor from two-thirty p.m. until five-thirty p.m. and had a private duty patient from seven p.m. until eleven p.m., all was Monday through Friday. Whewww, that was so much on me at once, but I felt that's what I had to do, and thank God I had help with my son being watched. I and JR eventually got another apartment together. Everything was starting to get back to normal. JR continued to do his thing, and I continued to do mine as we worked as a team. One year later, something wasn't feeling right with my body, a weird feeling that I had never experienced before, so I went to the emergency room. I was too uncomfortable; I just couldn't wait for a regular doctor's appointment. As I got to there, I explained to the doctor how I was feeling, got checked out for everything, found out JR had done giving me chlamydia and found out I had been pregnant again. As the doctor left the room, I was so hurt, thinking, why me? I was so scared because I had never gone through anything like this. Asking myself, what will I do with another child right now? This was another draining, stressful time of my life. Weeks later, I also found out that JR could have possibly had another child on the way besides mine. But come to find out that it was not his after the baby was born. I felt so relieved but felt so dumb. I was so dumb, and I was tired of all the bullshit with JR. Love had taken control of my mind. JR had me right where he wanted me. I just didn't know what was holding me back from moving on. Was I being blinded by the things he was providing for me? Was it the way he caressed my body? Was I scared of him moving on to better? One of JR's grandmothers (R.I.P) was such a sweet, loving woman; she would always preach to me that a man will only do what you allow them to do. I SHOULD HAVE LISTENED; I SHOULD HAVE LISTENED; I SHOULD HAVE LISTENED. I just wanted to be loved but looked for it from the wrong person. I continued helping JR stay on his feet when I could barely have helped myself. Eight months after the birth of my second child, I realized I wasn't comfortable with the amount of money I was making, so I ended up getting a job at the postal service with better pay and benefits. JR started wanting me to get rentals for him weekly, and I would get loans for him worth thousands of dollars just for him. I was willing to risk it all. I wasn't worried about me losing out on money because JR was a real hustler, and anything he would have borrowed, he flipped and made it back times two. JR started to get good inside the dope game where he would have started traveling for his work. He also started investing in his rapping career; I was there for it all. I was the type of girlfriend who would have literally done anything JR asked of me. At times, it got to the point; I would have put JR's needs and wants before my own kids' needs and wants, not realizing how I could have mentally affected them by not being around as much as I should have. Thankfully my parents weren't the type who didn't mind keeping their grands. I would jump on the road for him at any time of day, even if it took me to call out of work. JR made sure he always paid me for any days I would have missed from work plus the time I spent traveling up and down the highways bringing back all packs, meaning BIG boy packs, not even thinking or caring about the consequences I could have faced if I had got caught. Falling in love with the money, I just knew we were about to be super straight. JR then started calling me his "Road Angel," meaning me being a safe driver being his protection on the road while we both traveled. Making all the money JR started to make, I felt he started to get a little too Big-headed; things drastically changed. JR started not coming home every night and even talked to me differently at times; he claimed he didn't need me. JR must have forgotten who helped him out and who was there when he was down. It was like me and JR started having more and more arguments almost every day and fights more often, resulting in me having bust lips, black eyes, dragged, kicking, anything his mind would tell him to do. There was a time I really had to fake a seizure just for him to stop fighting me. I was tired of it all, and JR started to blame his actions on the use of coke. JR had one case of domestic violence on him, which I eventually dropped. One day I really got tired of his shit; he tried me, he took me out of my character, he knew how to get to me, he just knew if it had anything to do with another female, it would have irked my nerve, he really tried me this day. As we were arguing earlier that day, I decided to call him, no answer, so my phone rang suddenly, and it was JR. As I'm saying hello, he wasn't responding, so at this point, he had pocket dialed me, not realizing. I then heard some laughs in a female's voice, and then I heard JR saying, "You have to move your car because my grandaddy is on the way home."

I was heated; I hung up so fast, mad as hell not thinking before I was about to react; I jumped up and called my cousin so fast to take me over to where he was hoping he would still be there, I went and got this sharp ass steak knife out the kitchen, and I swear my cousin was to me in five minutes. We pulled up to the house, and there he was, standing in the yard. I jumped out of the car with the knife behind my back. I swear I did no talking; he's laughing, thinking it's a game while backing up from me; I'm walking towards him. I then ran up to him and just swung the knife and caught him on the side of the neck. Blood leaking all over, he tried to take the knife as we started to fight. I swore I had to have blacked out because all I felt was my cousin pulling me off of him. We then left; I had to snap back and pull myself back together. I couldn't believe I had just done that. I could have to kilt him. I could have hit an artery and really kilt this boy. JR's mother always knew about every confrontation I had, and he had only because of him. Believe it or not, JR was a real mama's boy; she knew everything that would go on between us. In some eyes, JR did no wrong.

Deep down inside, I felt like JR's mother would try to cover up his actions with excuses as to why he did this or what made him do that, but claimed he loved me so much. JR's mother knew the type of love I had for them, so being the manipulative type of person she was, I would always feel like it was my fault that caused JR to do the things he did. Everybody had their opinions but never been in my position. On the other hand, my parents knew of anything I was going through with JR. I was too embarrassed to speak to them about it, wishing I did because they probably could have saved me somehow. I was silently hurting mentally, physically, and emotionally by turning to the wrong people. There were days I would wake up and wish I had stayed asleep. There was no way I kept myself in such a dangerous relationship with such a ruthless individual. I had to get away, I wanted to get away, but I also wanted to stay. The day had finally come, the year 2014. I finally dared to leave. It was tough and so hard to ignore that we weren't together anymore. During this time of my life, I started wilding out; I was held down for so long that I didn't know how to act being free. I would go out to parties and clubs at least four times a week. I would drink almost every night, live and enjoy myself. I met this young man (R.I.P Tre D.) at the club one night, not even wanting to be bothered because of the shit I just got out of. He saw my name tattooed on my leg; it was funny because he searched me up on social media. He would constantly hit me up trying to get my attention, but I constantly would ignore him because, at that point, it was fuck a nigga. He didn't give up, and I gave in and gave him my number. We talked, and I suddenly began to have flashbacks because this is exactly how it started with JR, so I started to back off from him a little. He continued to send me sweet texts and decided to ask me out on a date, I really didn't want to, but ole boy wasn't giving up. Everything was the opposite of what I had assumed about him. He was such a good person with a nice personality. He would have done anything for me, accepted both of my kids. We spoke for about six months until JR started to ease his way back into my life. We started sneaking back around. Yeah, I was being stupid for JR again; it was like I was waiting for that moment to come. I and JR ended up back talking again. So many things started to go wrong for JR. JR was constantly getting in trouble with the law and was a target to many people. Unknown people would shoot at the cars he would be driving, and people would try to rob him; it was so scary. He was in danger, but I had also put myself and my kids back in a dangerous, unpredictable situation. Ten years into my and JR's relationship, he had a baby hidden from me for months. Once again, the other female and I were both pregnant at the same time (four months apart). As JR constantly would tell me back and forth, from it wasn't his, to he's not sure if it was his, I just knew he was lying. I then began to notice the change in his mother; she had blocked me off all her social media so that I wouldn't know or see when she posted the baby. She wouldn't get my kids when she had the other baby, and she wouldn't do as much as she would for my oldest two. I started to feel some type of way and confronted her about it, and she claimed she would do that to protect my feelings. So much was going on at the time; JR was getting ready to go up for court two months before my baby would have been born; on the other hand, JR was stressed out over the amount of time he was facing. Even though I was also going through a lot, I still managed to be there and stayed strong for him. I had decided to move back to my parents' house not only because JR's time was coming up to be convicted, but to get that little extra help still being pregnant, suffering from hypertension, not working, and still having to care for my other two kids. The day came, August 25, 2017. On court day, we all stood in the lobby area waiting for JR's time to go in. I was devastated; I cried so much as he repeatedly asked me not to leave him; I felt his nervousness as we held hands. As hours passed, it was JR's time to go up in front of the judge. The judge called JR up, read out his rights, and started to read out his charges. Wheww, my ears began to get numb; I then heard nine years. My heart dropped, leaving out with a horrible migraine. After being sentenced, JR was shipped back to the county jail, where he would get a couple of visitations until he got shipped to prison. After being shipped in the booking process, JR couldn't make phone calls for about six weeks. I felt lonely as I anxiously waited to hear his voice again. JR finally made his first phone call to me. I felt so sorry for him; I could have heard the regrets in his voice like he knew he had messed up. On October 17, 2017, I gave birth to my third child. I had so much support in my room, but it felt different because JR wasn't there. God places people in our lives at the right time. When JR got locked up, JR's best friend and his wife stepped up to be a part of me and my kids' lives to help me with my kids. They were so real and solid ever since and never left my side. I have so much love and respect for them as they are such a big blessing to us. Six weeks later, I finally started working, getting back in the swing of things. I made sure I had JR's back while incarcerated, putting minutes on the phone, money on his canteen, and any extra's he needed for other purposes. I promised JR I would have his back, and I had meant just that. Visitation time came around. I would drive an hour and a half there and back on Saturdays and Sundays to see him. I was so happy to get the chance to see him, touch him, to even kiss him again. I swear I didn't want to leave. JR was able to see my kids at visitation once before getting his rights taken away. As I surprised the kids and took them to see their father, they were so excited to see him after not seeing him for a whole year. They played board games with him, played cards, ate, and even took pictures. It was such a bittersweet moment and so emotional because our youngest child interacted with JR like he had known his father for years to say that was the first time they had ever met each other. I and JR would still have little arguments here and there. He started accusing me of cheating, telling lies about how he's hearing things about me in the streets. It was so funny to me that I knew he was lying because I literally just went to work daily and returned home to my kids. JR had too much time on his hands; I tried to be understanding, but he was starting to get out of hand. It was eating him up inside, and JR knew all the bullshit he had put me through when he was out, so, at this point, he was worried. JR started calling me every day to keep tabs on what I would be doing throughout the day. I still was faithful to a nigga who had put me through so much hell. I was the real definition of a "down ass bitch" One day, JR called me as I was taking a nap from a long day of work. Missing his phone call twice; as I woke up, I noticed the missed calls, and I was able to call the number back because he was using a roommate's phone. I called the number back, and JR answered. "Aye yo, you ain't seeing me calling you. I responded, "Well, damn, I was sleeping, JR. I can't catch every call" He then hung up. JR knew I couldn't stand being hanged up on, so I called back. JR decided to push the ignore button, causing me to call back multiple times until he answered. JR finally decided to answer, so as I tried to explain myself, he just wasn't trying to believe me. I started thinking to myself, why am I so intimidated by him? JR then told me to stop calling the phone and be a hoe like I had been. He then said that nobody was going to want me with three kids. JR was spazzing out on me for no apparent reason. The last thing JR said to me this day that shocked me was, "go find somebody else to talk to; why are you worrying about a nigga that's in jail. Believe it or not, that day year 2019, I made up my mind to move on to make myself happy again. I left for good this time.

JR is really NEVER going to change. It was such a big relief for me. Throughout the years, I was worn out from JR, holding things inside and dealing with them. Nobody really understands or knows what a person goes through daily. I started to get myself together in many ways and did what was best for my kids and me. People started to tell me they would see a glow in me; that made me feel so good inside because that was just my confirmation that I was on the path of doing the right thing. I couldn't believe I spent most of my young age caught up in a no-good situation, playing housewife to someone who meant no good to me and only cared about what I could have provided for him. They say everything happens for a reason. Everything had to happen exactly how it did just for me to get where God was leading me next. It was meant for JR to be sentenced. It was my only way out. I promised never to put myself or my kids back through anything like this again. I prayed my way out of this for so long. I had spent years painting a picture that wasn't even there. I'm so proud to say I am a domestic violence survivor. It could have been worse, but God had a purpose for me. People take things for granted until their in that situation, but I will never laugh at another female's hurt. There was no communication between me and JR. My life was so peaceful; no worries, no being used, and no having to spend extra unnecessary money. I was actually enjoying my life, and I was in my healing stage. It took me two years to get back on track, and I didn't want to be bothered by any nigga. I loved my kids more than ever. Months later, JR called me out of the blue; there was no type of anger or hate against him; I just wasn't about to play with him any longer. I was tired of hearing apologies; my mind was already set on never going back to that dark place I was in. JR and I weren't together, but he would call just to check up on the kids and me. JR knew I had a soft spot for him, so I had to be strong and block out the sweet talks he would often speak. I moved on to better, met someone who cared for me and all three of my kids, brought our first home in 2021, and had a beautiful baby girl. As JR was still often calling to check in, I didn't want to mention anything to him about my pregnancy because he was going through a family issue at the time instead of dealing with his problems. JR then found out I was pregnant, asked me about it, and I told him the truth that I was. JR was mad and hurt and wanted me to abort my child. I couldn't; I just couldn't. The hurt in his voice as he said to me, "I can kill you right now" His anger spoke out loud, but I knew for sure JR wouldn't change from that moment. After not hearing from JR for a couple of days, he decided to call; we spoke; he explained his emotions and feelings and apologized for what he had said. JR also mentioned that a couple of his family members didn't want him talking to me anymore because I had a baby on the way, and they claimed that I purposely did that to hurt him. What was said didn't surprise me because I'm sure I know the ones who actually said it. I'm not saying I intentionally got pregnant, but nothing was said when it was the other way around. I have learned that people will always have something to say regardless of any situation. JR felt like he was stuck between listening to family versus wanting to make things right with his created family. I couldn't do it with him anymore after thirteen years of dealing with hurt, pain, lies, abuse, and problems with his mother numerous times. I HONESTLY JUST COULDN'T DO IT ANYMORE. JR knew he had an awesome woman and a great mother to his kids, but when it all came down to the conclusion, JR felt When Hurt Hits.

MOTIVATIONAL SPEECH

Many of us have hidden stories we are afraid to come out to make known to people. I'm here to tell you it is ok. I have been there also. Don't be afraid to leave. I realized that I was living in that fear. Leaving in fear of him leaving me, fear of not knowing if I would have survived, fear of my family finding out. However, this is crazy to say. I never was afraid when I was taking penitentiary chances for him, and that was because I didn't love me enough. How could I ever want and love something so bad that was constantly hurting me. On my road to escaping my domestic violence relationship, I found myself, I found love, and most importantly, I found purpose.

Domestic violence statistics 42.3% of South Carolina women and 29.2% of South Carolinian men experience intimate partner physical violence. In 2019 36 women and 6 men were victims of domestic violence homicide. 78.5% of these homicides were committed with firearms. On a single day in 2020, South Carolina domestic violence hotlines received 21,321 calls, an average of almost 15 calls every minute. 65% of all murder-suicides involve an intimate partner, and 96% of the victims of these crimes are females. In the year 2022, South Carolina ranks seventh among all states concerning the percentage of females who experienced intimate partner violence at some point during their lifetime.

CPSIA information can be obtained
at www.ICGtesting.com
Printed in the USA
BVHW050635160522
637110BV00014B/447